Osvaldo Golijov

Azul

Solo Violoncello Part

HENDON MUSIC

7777 W. BLUEMOUND RD. P.O. BOX 13819 MILWAUKEE, WI 53213

www.boosey.com
www.halleonard.com

VIOLONCELLO SOLO

Para Alicia

AZUL

I. Paz Sulfúrica

Osvaldo Golijov

V.S.

Rev. Oct. 2013

VIOLONCELLO SOLO

subito meno ***f***, retaking energy

112–115

attacca

II. Silencio

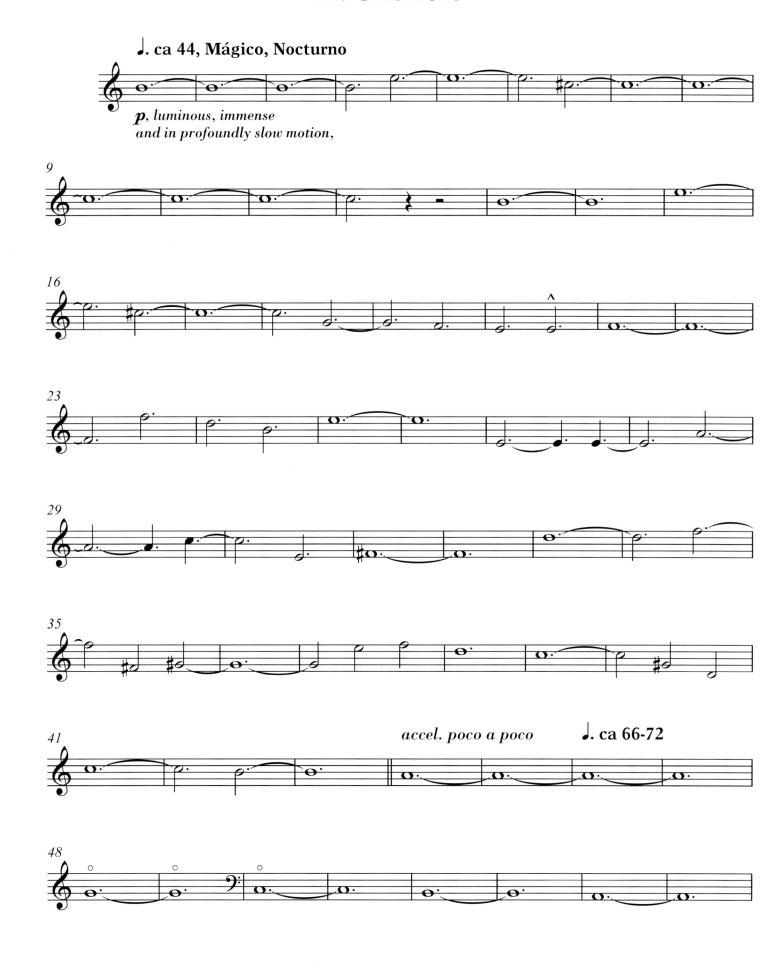

III. Transit

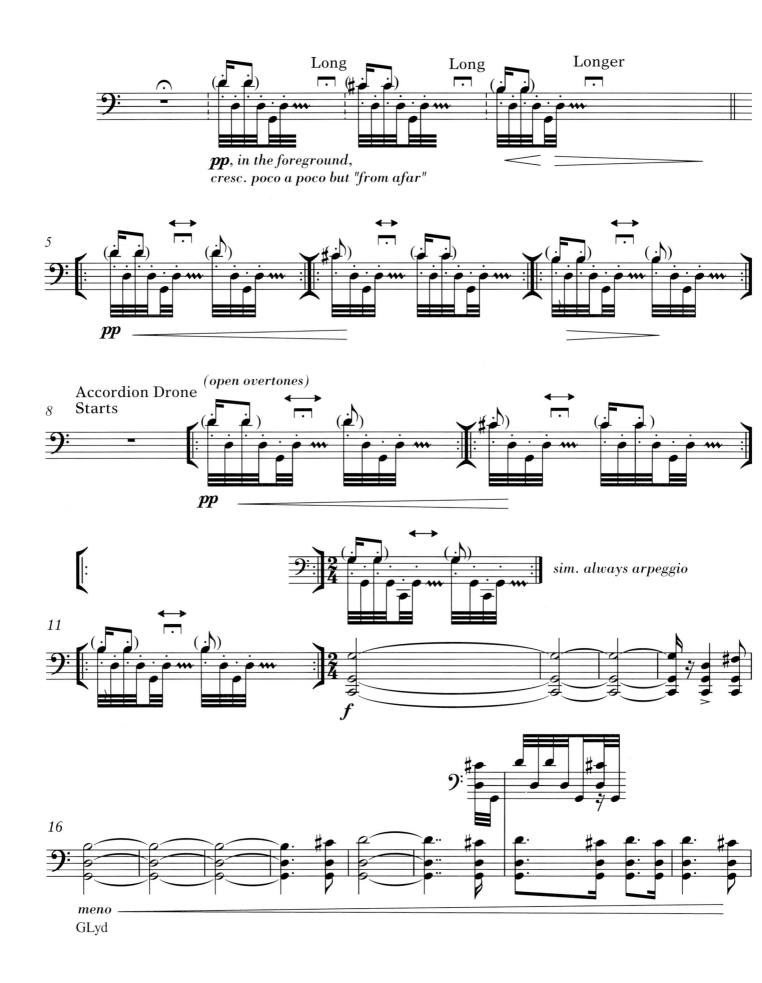

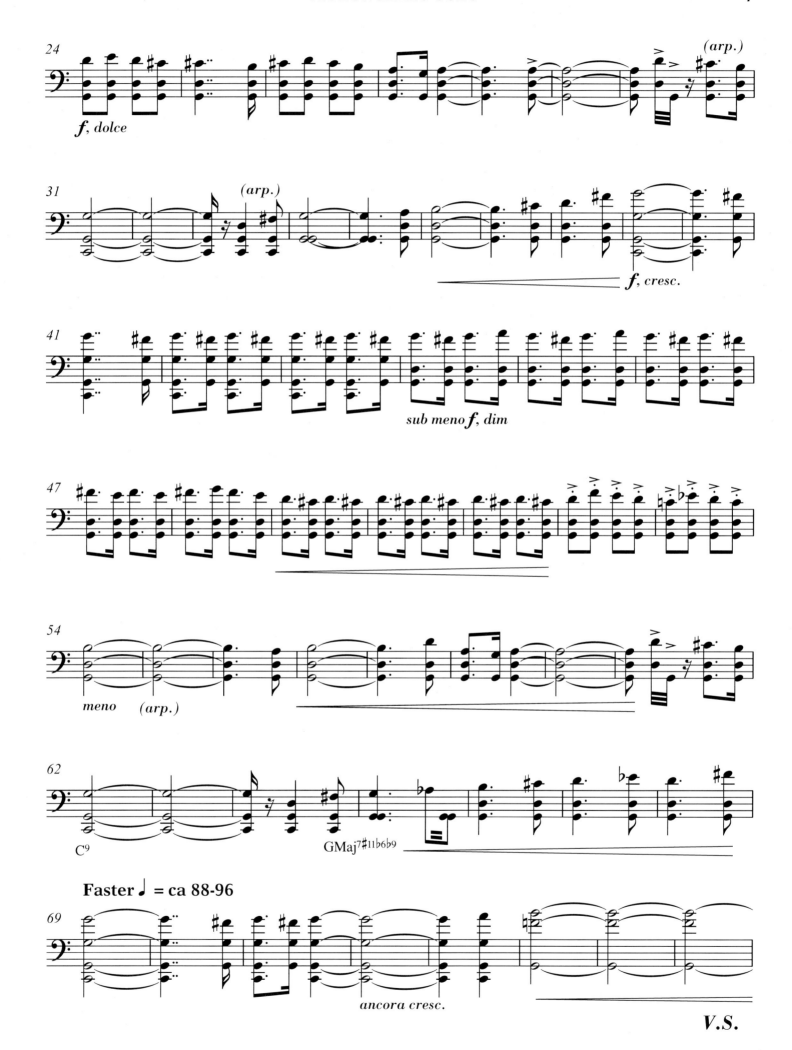

V.S.

Magic

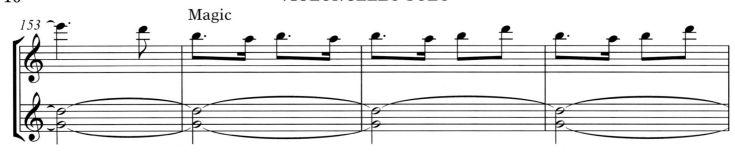

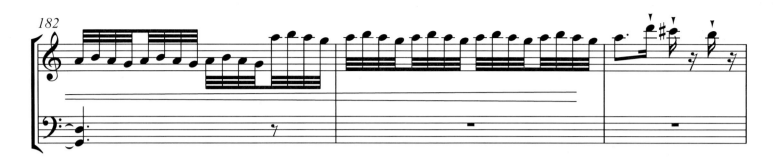

attacca

IV. Yrushalem

Cl., Bs. Hn.

like prayer fragments

PLAY

Yer - u - sha - lem

cresc. poco a poco

CODA I: PULSAR

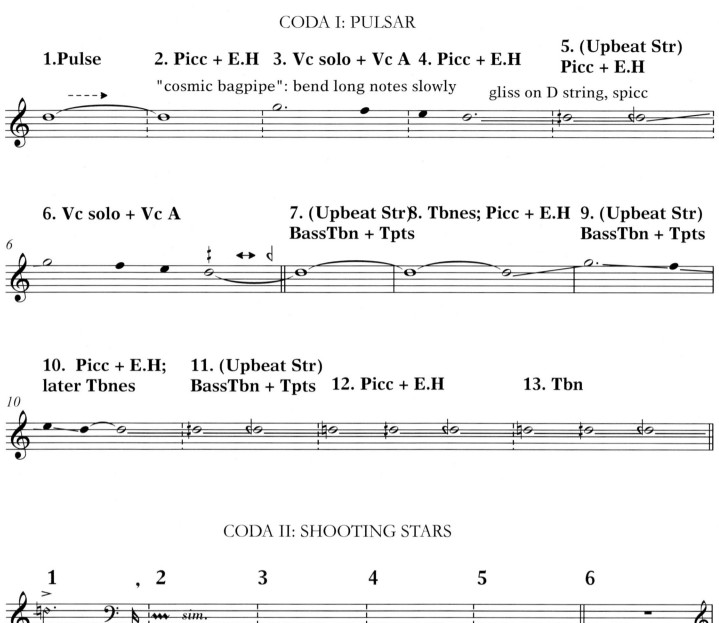

CODA II: SHOOTING STARS

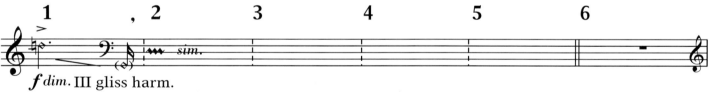